LONDON BOROUGH OF ENFIELD
SCHOOLS LIBRARY SERVICE

91200000364034

| PETERS | 18-Feb-2015 |
| | 940.531 |

Stories of World War II
KINDERTRANSPORT

By A. J. Stones

WAYLAND

First published in 2014 by Wayland
Copyright © Wayland 2014

Wayland
338 Euston Road
London NW1 3BH

Wayland Australia
Level 17/207 Kent Street
Sydney, NSW 2000

Editor: Elizabeth Brent
Designer: Elaine Wilkinson
Researchers: Hester Vaizey, Edward Field and Ela Kaczmarska
at The National Archives

The National Archives, London, England.
www.nationalarchives.gov.uk

The National Archives looks after the UK government's historical documents. It holds records dating back nearly 1,000 years from the time of William the Conqueror's Domesday Book to the present day. All sorts of documents are stored there, including letters, photographs, maps and posters. They include records of great Kings and Queens, famous rebels like Guy Fawkes and the strange and unusual – such as reports of UFOs and even a mummified rat!

Picture credits: Front cover © Getty Images (tr, tl), © Mary Evans Picture Library/Imagno (b); back cover © Bea Green; p1 ©The Wiener Library; p2–3 © Getty Images; p4 © Imperial War Museums (FRA 204717); p5 © Getty Images (t), Shutterstock.com/Elzbieta Sekowska (b); p6 © Imperial War Museums (HU 8482) (t), © Shutterstock.com/Naci Yavuz (b); p7 © Imperial War Museums (GER 305) (t), © Bettmann/CORBIS (b); p8 © Ferdinand Vitzethum/ Sammlung Superikonoskop; p9 © George Grantham Bain Collection; p10 © Imperial War Museums (EPH 3902) (t), Getty Images (b); p11 © Bea Green (t), © Imperial War Museums (EPH 8469) (m), © Imperial War Museums (EPH 3918) (b); p12 © Getty Images; p13 ©The Wiener Library, p14 © Getty Images; p15 © Getty Images (t), Shutterstock.com/ JuliusKielaitis (b); p16 © Getty Images (t), ©The Wiener Library (b); p17 © REX/The Weiner Library; p18 © Shutterstock.com/Baloncici (t), © IWM via Getty Images (t); p19 © REX/The Weiner Library; p20 © REX/The Weiner Library; p21 © Getty Images; p22 © REX/The Weiner Library (t), Getty Images (b); p23 © Imperial War Museums (EA 63141); p24 © Imperial War Museums (HU 3266) (t), © Imperial War Museums (HU 36121) (b); p25 © Getty Images; p26 © REX/Associated Newspapers; p27 © Heritage Images/ Getty Images; p28 © Imperial War Museums (D 24586); p29 © Markus Pössel (t), ©The National Archives (b); p32 © Getty Images (t), © Imperial War Museums (HU 36121) (b).

Background and graphic elements courtesy of Shutterstock.

Disclaimer: Every effort has been made to trace the copyright holder but if you feel you have the rights to any images contained in this book then please contact the publisher.

Please note:
The website addresses (URLs) included in this book were valid at the time of going to press. However, because of the nature of the Internet, it is possible that some addresses may have changed, or sites may have changed or closed down since publication. While the author and publishers regret any inconvenience this may cause to the readers, no responsibility for such changes can be accepted by either the author or the publishers.

A cataloguing record for this title is available at the British Library.

ISBN 978 0 7502 7963 5
Ebook ISBN 978 0 7502 8836 1

10 9 8 7 6 5 4 3 2 1

Dewey Number 940.5'3161-dc23

Printed in China

Wayland is a division of Hachette Children's Books,
an Hachette UK company
www.hachette.co.uk

CONTENTS

What was Kindertransport?	4
Life under the Nazis	6
Planning the Transport	8
Leaving Germany	10
Arriving in England	12
Dovercourt Camp	14
Daily routine	16
Moving on	18
Culture shock	20
The Transport ends	22
Under suspicion	24
Adopted by Britain	26
The end of the war	28
Glossary	30
Further reading	31
Index	32

What was Kindertransport?

Kindertransport was the name given to a large rescue mission that took place during World War II. Between 1938 and 1940, thousands of Jewish children were taken from Nazi Germany and brought to safety in Great Britain. The name is a combination of 'Kinder', the German word for children, and the English word 'transport'.

Why were the Jews at risk?

Adolf Hitler was appointed Chancellor of Germany on 30th January 1933. He was leader of the anti-Semitic Nazi Party, which created laws designed to make life difficult for Jewish people. In 1938, the Nazis began a series of attacks on Jewish families in Germany. The worst was called Kristallnacht, or 'Crystal Night', on 9th–10th November 1938. Jews were attacked in the street and arrested for no reason, and many of their shops and homes were burned down.

The ruins of a synagogue in Berlin, destroyed during Kristallnacht.

Bringing the children to safety

The Jewish people in Germany needed protecting, so the British government organised trains and boats to bring German-Jewish children to Great Britain. The transportation was planned by a new organisation called 'The Movement For The Care Of Children From Germany'. This voluntary group was made up of members of various religious organisations including Jews, Quakers and Christians. They later changed their name to the 'Refugee Children's Movement' (RCM) when they began to evacuate Jewish children from other countries that had been invaded by the Nazis – mainly Czechoslovakia, Poland and Austria.

Thousands arrive in Britain

The Movement worked quickly and the first children arrived in Britain just three weeks after Kristallnacht. The trains continued to leave from Germany until World War II began on 1 September 1939. By then, around 10,000 children had been transported. Their parents and guardians had to stay behind; most of them would never see their children again.

A ship carrying Kinder arrives in England on 2nd December 1938.

ADOLF HITLER

Adolf Hitler blamed the Jews for all of Germany's problems, including the country losing World War I. He wanted to create a 'master race', and remove anyone he considered inferior. At first, he sent Jewish people out of the country, but by the end of World War II he had ordered the deaths of millions of Jewish men, women and children.

Life under the Nazis

When he came to power in 1933, Hitler began passing laws to make life hard for the Jewish population. He bombarded the German people with large amounts of information representing Jews as evil and untrustworthy people. It became harder and harder for Jews to keep their friends and business partners, because no one wanted to be associated with them.

Propaganda

The Nazi Party used propaganda to portray Hitler as Germany's saviour and spread his criticism of Jewish people. Pictures of him were placed in schools and offices and the Nazi flag was hung from public buildings. Hitler's speeches were also broadcast on the radio and from speakers in the streets. *Der Stürmer*, an anti-Jewish newspaper, explained how to spot Jewish criminals and published cartoons of Jews with evil, twisted faces.

The main train station in Berlin was decorated with Nazi flags during the 1930s.

Jews were forced to mark their clothes and shops with the Star of David.

Bullied on the streets

From 1933, the Nazis banned Jews from using certain public spaces. They were forced to sit apart from other train and bus passengers and could use only specially marked park benches. Jewish children were placed in separate classrooms and bullying them was permitted. Jews weren't allowed to play for their schools' sports teams. By 1934, all Jewish shops were marked with the word *Juden* (German for Jews) or a yellow Star of David. Nazis stood outside the shop doors and stopped any non-Jews from going inside. Other shop owners were not allowed to sell food or medicine to Jews. Jewish men were sacked from their jobs and eventually Jewish children were banned completely from attending school or university.

Taken without warning

In 1935, the Nuremberg Law was passed, which meant that Jews were no longer considered to be German citizens. Jews were forbidden from marrying non-Jews and they lost all their legal rights. The richest families paid a fine to leave the country, but those who remained were at serious risk. Jewish men began to disappear, often taken without warning in the middle of the night. In October 1939, around 18,000 Jews were deported from Poland, and forced to find a new place to live.

Cartoons in children's school books presented Jews as cruel thieves.

KRISTALLNACHT

Kristallnacht, or 'Crystal Night', took place over 9th and 10th November 1938. Nazi soldiers killed more than 90 Jews and sent another 30,000 to concentration camps. They also ransacked synagogues and set fire to buildings owned by or associated with Jewish people, leaving the streets covered in shards of crystal-like glass from their windows.

Planning the Transport

In 1933 there were around 500,000 Jews in Germany, making up less than 1% of the population. More than 35,000 Jews left when the Nazis came to power. Thousands more decided to join them as their living conditions worsened. Those who stayed needed help, but the other European countries had problems of their own.

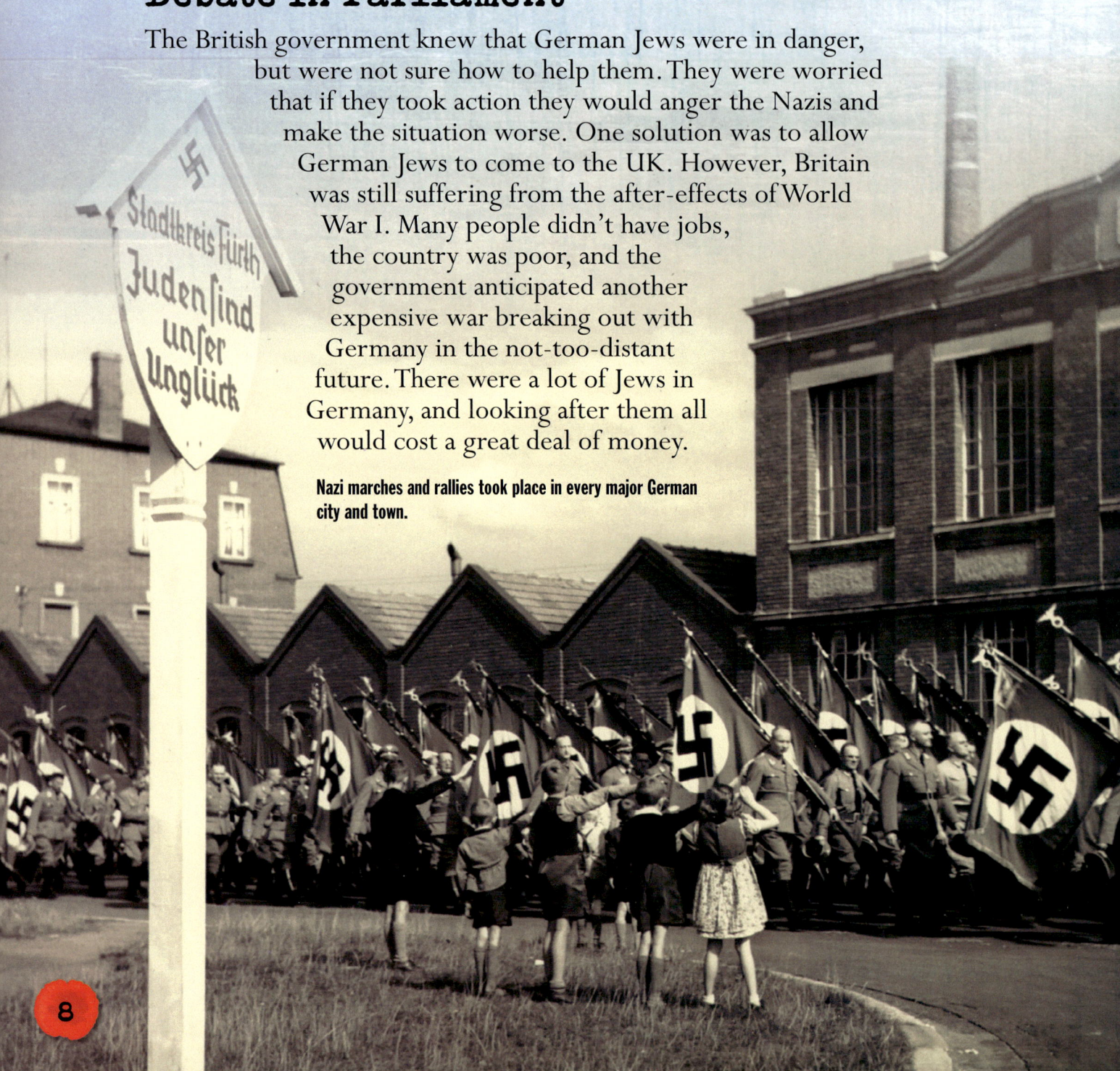

Debate in Parliament

The British government knew that German Jews were in danger, but were not sure how to help them. They were worried that if they took action they would anger the Nazis and make the situation worse. One solution was to allow German Jews to come to the UK. However, Britain was still suffering from the after-effects of World War I. Many people didn't have jobs, the country was poor, and the government anticipated another expensive war breaking out with Germany in the not-too-distant future. There were a lot of Jews in Germany, and looking after them all would cost a great deal of money.

Nazi marches and rallies took place in every major German city and town.

Returning home

On 25th November 1938, the BBC launched a radio appeal for foster families. Adverts for sponsors were also placed in *The Jewish Chronicle* and other newspapers. Sponsors were needed because the plan was ultimately to reunite each child with its parents, so every child required a donation of £50 (around £1,400 today) to cover their return travel. It was not essential for the foster families to be Jewish, and offers soon came in. Refugee Children's Movement (RCM) members began visiting the possible homes and reporting back to the government.

BRITISH SYMPATHY

British sympathy was high and many families were keen to help the unfortunate children. In a letter at the time, Mr J. Harker, of Halifax in Yorkshire, wrote to the Foreign Secretary, Lord Halifax, "I am deeply concerned for the plight of young German girls and boys, who, after leaving school find life more intolerable for them owing to the racial and religious differences in their own country."

Changing the rules

After Kristallnacht, the RCM spoke to Samuel Hoare, the Home Secretary. Hoare became their strongest supporter and took their ideas to the House of Commons. He asked that Jewish children of 17 and younger be allowed to enter the country on a temporary basis. The government agreed and lifted visa and passport restrictions. This meant the children could arrive in the UK without the usual documents. All they needed was a specially made white card.

Sir Samuel Hoare asked the government to help the German Jewish children.

Leaving Germany

The Kindertransport scheme had to be organised in a hurry. The Nazis wanted the Jews to leave, but they didn't allow them to go from German ports. The children had to travel on trains to the Netherlands and Belgium before catching ferries to Britain.

Groups of Kinder caught trains in Vienna bound for Liverpool Street station in London.

Choosing the children

The RCM sent volunteers to Germany and Austria to choose, organise and deliver the children to the correct trains. The Quaker members of the movement were the most involved and often stayed with the children throughout the long journey. Priority was given to the most vulnerable children – orphans, the homeless, those whose parents were under attack for standing up to the Nazi Party, or those who were already in concentration camps.

Saying goodbye

Parents knew they might be separated from their children for a long time. They couldn't promise that they would be able to follow them and a lot of the Kinder were too young to understand what was happening. The Quakers placed the children on the trains and made sure the youngest were looked after by the older travellers. As they left their parents, elder siblings suddenly found themselves in charge of distressed younger brothers and sisters.

A group of Kinder leave Munich station for England in June 1937.

Packing up

The Nazi government limited the children to one suitcase and one backpack each. They were allowed to take 10 marks, which was worth 84 pence in England (just over £10 today). The children could take only items for personal use, and were banned from packing any jewellery, musical instruments or cameras. To save space in their bags, the children often put on as many clothes as possible. It might be hot under two coats and three shirts, but they would be useful later. Others dressed in their very best clothes. Many Kinder gathered small items like teddy bears and pillows to remind them of home. Some, however, had to leave in such a hurry they didn't take anything. Everyone was given a tag with a number and their name on it, and an identity card to help the RCM place them on the correct train.

QUAKERS

The Quaker Movement is also known as The Society of Friends. They consider themselves Christian but share many different beliefs. They are united by their commitment to peace, truth and equality.

11

Arriving in England

The first Kindertransport arrived in England on 2nd December 1938. A ferry reached the port of Harwich with 196 orphans on board. Transports arrived every week after this, with only a few days' rest over the Easter holiday in 1939.

Over land and sea

The children caught trains from major European cities such as Vienna, Berlin and Prague. When they arrived in Belgium and The Netherlands, they caught ships to England. Some children took a plane from Czechoslovakia to Great Britain, and at least one transport left directly from Germany. The SS *Europa* left the German city of Bremen on 13th June 1939, dropping young refugees in Southampton on its way to New York in the USA.

RCM members checked the identity tags of the Kinder on arrival in England.

The holding camps

On arrival in England, children were taken to specially prepared camps before they were sent to their new homes. The camps of Dovercourt, in Essex, and Lowestoft, in Suffolk, were two of the biggest. They contained rows of small concrete huts with wooden floors. Each hut held several bunks, a cupboard and a chest. There was also one larger building with a hall, where everyone ate and spent their spare time. When the children arrived they were interviewed and given a thorough medical examination. All of their details, including their name, age and date of arrival, were kept in a separate office on the site.

New homes

The children who already had sponsors were called 'the guaranteed' and were taken to their new homes as quickly as possible. However, the majority of the Kinder arrived without a sponsor. They were called 'the unguaranteed' and had to stay in the camps until a home could be found for them. Around half of the children who arrived in England ended up living with foster families. The others stayed in hostels, boarding schools or farms throughout the country. Some were sent overseas, with more than 800 children travelling to the safer lands of the USA, Canada and Australia.

Kinder stand outside their rooms at Dovercourt Camp in December 1938.

NICHOLAS WINTON

In 1938, Nicholas Winton was a 29-year-old stockbroker living in London. He had planned to go skiing in Switzerland that winter, but flew to Prague instead. He set up an office in a hotel and put all of his efforts into saving Czech children from the Nazis. In the nine months before the outbreak of war, he saved 664 children.

Dovercourt Camp

The camp at Dovercourt originally belonged to The Butlins Company. It was built as a summer destination, where people on holiday could rent out huts. During World War II, however, boys and girls between five and 18 years old lived there. In total, 350 children were kept in the camp.

Schoolboys from Eton teach a song to a group of Kinder at Dovercourt Camp.

Staff and volunteers

The leader of the camp was a nursery school headmaster called Mr M.J. Banks. All members of staff were volunteers and many were refugees themselves. They looked after around 10 children each, and sat with them during meals. Every evening, they held a roll call. Public school boys and young children from the local area came in to help for a few weeks at a time. Doctors from Austria cared for the sick and injured, and a hairdresser cut the children's hair on her days off.

Four meals a day

The catering was provided by Butlins. They employed four cooks and a handful of stewards in their kitchen. The food was bought locally at the cost of £1 per head a week (about £29 in today's money). A standard breakfast consisted of cocoa, porridge, bread and butter. At lunch, staff and children were given a hot meal of boiled mutton, fried fish and chips, shepherd's pie or mixed vegetables. Puddings included boiled rice with currants, jam rolls and syrup pudding. The evening meal was usually a small, cold one, nothing more than a cup of tea, bread, butter and fruit. A government report described the camp's food as 'of the most ordinary kind.'

A group of Kinder are given their first meal on arrival at Dovercourt Camp.

A harsh winter

The camps were extremely cold in the winter, especially in December. The huts were not heated and only the main hall had a stove. This meant that there was only one warm building, and the children had to sleep in the cold. Each child was provided with a hot water bottle and five blankets. In 1938, Dovercourt froze completely and the children had to be sent more than 100 kilometres away to a girls' school in Lowestoft.

CLOTHES

The clothes at Dovercourt were donated by Marks and Spencer's, whose shops can still be seen on high streets today. The camp kept them in a clothing store and distributed coats, jerseys, dressing gowns and boots as and when children needed them.

Daily routine

It was difficult to plan a child's time in the camps, because the staff didn't know how long each child would be staying for. The Kinder left as soon as they had a sponsor and were replaced by new arrivals. Their days were often unstructured, with few organised activities.

Duties and chores

The Kinder were responsible for making their own beds and cleaning their huts. The older children helped organise the younger ones to scrub out the main shared building and get their own food at mealtimes. The older children had lessons in the morning, which concentrated on learning English for their stay in the country. The young children simply drew pictures and sang songs. In the afternoon, the older boys played football outside, while everyone else went for walks, practised their sewing or wrote letters.

The Kinder had to study hard to learn English.

Spare time

Between lessons and mealtimes, the children were left to create their own entertainment. They played board games and talked. Sometimes the children would place all their drawings on a wall, creating their own art exhibition. If there was a piano, they could practise their music. Some camps also had an outdoor swimming pool, which the children were free to use in summer.

Kinder played with whatever toys where available in the camps.

16

Leaving the camp

A selection of the children left the camp in the afternoon and visited nearby villages. In Harwich, local families drove to the camp and took the Kinder to their houses for tea. For many, this was the first time they had seen the inside of an English home. Conversation would have been very difficult, but the scones, jam tarts and cakes they were offered were a real treat. The families then dropped the Kinder back at the camp, perhaps with a bar of chocolate to share with their friends.

The Kinder had to share rooms with children they may never have met before.

SINGING AND PERFORMING

Some cinemas invited the Kinder to watch the most recent releases, including animated films such as Disney's *Snow White*. These trips were rare, however, so the camps put on their own shows. Most camps had a stage in the main building and the children rehearsed and performed their own plays and concerts. Local talent also volunteered to amuse the children.

Moving on

The Kinder who found sponsors were sent to their new homes. Foster parents were usually fairly well off and came from all over the United Kingdom. The RCM were not worried if the sponsors were Jewish or not – the most important thing was that the Kinder had a roof over their head and food in their stomach.

Different houses

The usual destination for children leaving the camps was Liverpool Street Station in London. From London they could catch a train to anywhere in the country. Kinder lived in the spare rooms of private houses, or in space within larger country houses that had been offered to the RCM. Barham House in Broadstairs, Kent was just one of these houses, and took in 40 boys. Their kitchen served kosher food, and the boys were given sixpence a week (70p today) as pocket money.

A memorial to the Kinder still stands outside Liverpool Street Station.

Learning new skills

Other stately homes were used to train the children for important jobs. Although they were not expected to stay in Britain for ever, some of the older children were already approaching working age. Jewish communities in places like Manchester and Belfast provided agricultural and mechanical training. Many of the Kinder proved to be highly skilled and were employed in the local area.

An evacuee feeds pigs on a farm in Devon.

Engeham Farm Camp

One of the largest centres for agricultural training was the farm camp in Engeham, Kent. More than 100 children were looked after by 15 adults. The living arrangements were very basic. Everyone lived in tents and slept on mattresses on a ground sheet. In the winter, they converted old railway carriages into dormitories. They bathed at the local lido and had to send their clothes to a nearby town to be cleaned. The children were woken at 6am every day. They ate a quick breakfast, then worked on the farm. Jobs included cutting hedges, milking cows, ploughing fields and planting seeds.

POPULAR VISITORS

On 18th September 1942, the *Evening Standard* explained how 34 Kinder working at a farm camp near Worcester had become popular with the local community. Many of them were the sons and daughters of doctors, dentists or lawyers. One 15-year-old boy was a particular favourite because he sang opera while driving his tractor.

Culture shock

The government was worried about overcrowding towns and villages, so they spread the Kinder throughout the country. The Jewish children came from completely different cultures and some struggled to fit in with their new neighbours.

Making friends

At first, the Kinder found it hard to make friends. They were often bullied because their European features, accents and clothes made them stand out. However, it didn't take them long to bond with the local children over games and food. The Kinder shared their stories of the camps and the journey, while the British children gave them advice, like which deals were best at the sweet shop.

Meals were an important time for the Kinder to bond with their hosts.

SOLOMON SCHONFELD

Solomon Schonfeld was the son-in-law of the Chief Rabbi in Britain during World War II. He supported the Kindertransport scheme and ran a Jewish school in London. He was worried that Jewish children would be converted to other religions while living in the UK and taught his students to become teachers and leaders in local Jewish communities.

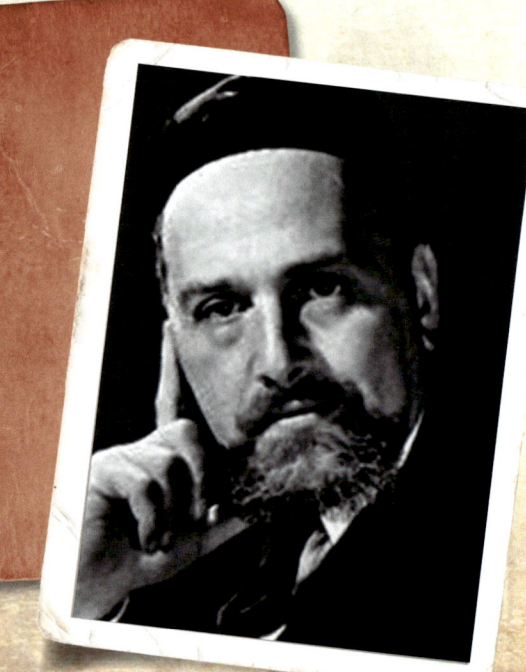

Language barrier

Most of the Kinder did not know much English, and any they did know they spoke with a foreign accent. If the lessons at the camp weren't enough, the Kinder had to practise their English on their own, until they could manage at school. Despite their difficulties, the Kinder were very good at learning new skills. The boys were trained in practical work like farming and tailoring, while the girls made dresses and got jobs as maids and cooks. Many Kinder also went to university.

The Kinder got together to celebrate Jewish holidays such as Hannukah.

Keeping the faith

The RCM were very clear that the Kinders' religion must be accepted by their hosts, and that the hosts were not allowed to try and convert the children. Due to the shortage of Jewish homes, it became important to find ways for the Kinder to worship. They were put in touch with local rabbis, who visited or wrote to them. Special trips were organised so that the Kinder could attend the nearest synagogue.

The Transport ends

Germany closed its borders in the months before World War II began. The Kindertransport scheme was seriously affected, because trains could no longer leave the country. The ships continued sailing from Belgium and the Netherlands until the Nazis invaded those countries in May 1940.

The last Transport

The very last Kindertransport ship to leave mainland Europe was called the *Bodegraven*. The Transport left the port of Ymuiden in the Netherlands on 14th May 1940. Rotterdam was bombed on the same day and the *Bodegraven* escaped under fire from the Luftwaffe, the German Air Force. Holland surrendered just a day later and the transport scheme officially ended. Hundreds of children were stranded in Belgium and the Netherlands, with no way of getting home.

The last Kinder ships became the only way to escape Europe.

Here to stay

When Britain declared war on Germany on 3rd September 1939, the RCM had to change their plans. It was impossible to send the children back to their home countries while the danger remained. The treatment of Jews in Europe was becoming much worse, and Britain was one of the only safe places left for them to stay. Around 10,000 Kinder were now expected to remain in the UK for the foreseeable future, and the government had to find a way of looking after them.

Two Jewish children in Poland in 1944. Life was very tough for Jews in mainland Europe during World War II.

Jews in Europe were sent to concentration camps and suffered terrible conditions.

Needing care

Every area of the country was given a special blue book. It contained instructions for regional and local committees on how to look after the Kinder. It stressed how important it was that they all had somewhere to stay and that they were cared for, because they had suffered terrible experiences. All of the children had been moved away from their families, and anyone they knew remaining in mainland Europe was at risk of death at the hands of the Nazis.

THE HOLOCAUST

The Kinder were saved from a terrible fate. In 1933, there were 9 million Jews in Europe. The Nazis killed around 6 million of them — by 1945, nearly two out of every three Jews in Europe had been killed. This highly organised and large-scale murder is known as the Holocaust.

Under suspicion

German forces began their invasion of France on 10th May 1940. Just over a month later, on 14th June, Nazi troops marched into Paris. With Britain's closest ally under German control, the fear of invasion grew stronger. Any person from overseas was viewed with suspicion, including the Kinder.

Hitler posed for a photo in front of the Eiffel Tower after his troops entered Paris.

Threat of invasion

To protect Britain from invasion, any foreign people over the age of 16 were registered as 'enemy aliens'. The government needed to be certain that no one in the country was spying for the Germans. Any men and women who were not born as British citizens were sent to camps for questioning. These internment camps were spread across the country, with the largest on the Isle of Man. Around 10,000 children, many of them Kinder, were kept in these camps.

Some Kinder were sent to internment camps on the Isle of Man.

Warth Mill

Warth Mill, in Bury near Manchester, was a large cotton mill that was used as an internment camp. Four thousand 'enemy aliens' were forced to sleep on its floor, surrounded by oily cotton waste. There were no washing facilities and barrels in the hall had to be used as toilets. Many of the people in the mill had been in England for a long time, having fled Germany before World War I.

Sent abroad

As well as keeping foreigners in camps, the government organised ships to take them out of the country. Every passenger's name, birthday and date of arrival in Britain was written down. However, this was a large undertaking and mistakes were made. In the confusion, around 400 Kinder were sent to Australia and Canada by accident. They had to endure awful conditions on the ships – everywhere was crowded, and there wasn't enough food to go round.

British soldiers guarded the internment camps.

SS ARANDORA STAR

Foreigners continued to be sent abroad until the SS *Arandora Star* set sail in June 1940. It was sunk by a German U-boat and the 800 people on board lost their lives. After this, the government stopped sending the internees away.

Adopted by Britain

Once it became clear that the Kinder had little chance of returning home, the government had to decide how to look after them. All of the Kinder had travelled without their parents and had no family to take responsibility for them.

The Guardianship Act

All of the children under the age of 18 needed a legal guardian — an adult to sign for important things like hospital treatment. This was a difficult situation for the government, because there were thousands of Kinder, and it would have been almost impossible to find legal guardians for all of them. The answer came with the creation of the Guardianship Act (for refugee children) in 1944. Lord Gorell, the chairman of the Refugee Children's Movement, was announced as the guardian of all the Kinder in Britain. He effectively adopted them all. This was the first time that someone had become the guardian of a group of people.

LORD GORELL

Ronald Gorell Barnes was a remarkable man. He was educated at Oxford University and played professional cricket for 13 seasons. He became a lawyer and also worked as a journalist for *The Times*. During World War I he was a captain in the Rifle Brigade and received the Military Cross. He was also co-president of the Detection Club with the author Agatha Christie.

Joining the Forces

During the war, a large number of the Jewish refugees turned 18. They were now legally adults and many joined the British army. Their first-hand knowledge of Europe and understanding of the German language meant that they were well suited to elite units such as the Special Forces. The Royal Pioneer Corps and auxiliary services were also popular choices for the new recruits. Those who didn't join the forces contributed to the war effort in other ways, through factory work, or by becoming a nurse, for example. Some Kinder were keen to join the fighting because their families had suffered at the hands of the Nazis. They wanted the war to be over as quickly as possible, so they could return home. Other Kinder simply didn't know what else they could do, and still more wanted to thank the British people for giving them a new home.

Volunteers join the British Army in Palestine in 1944. Many Jews enlisted as soldiers to fight the Nazis.

The end of the war

8th May 1945 was a happy day for most of Europe. Known as Victory in Europe (VE) Day, it was a celebration of the war's end. However, some Kinder had been away from their families for more than five years. The end of the war was certain to bring sad or unwelcome news.

Finding their family

By the time the Guardianship Act was introduced, some Kinder had been in Britain for five years. Many were old enough to work, and had settled into their new lives. When the war ended all Kinder were given a card with the name and last known address of their parents. It was incredibly difficult to trace missing relatives, because of the small amount of information available. Jewish families in Europe were unlikely to be in the same house they had been living in before the outbreak of war, and there was also the possibility they had been sent to a concentration camp.

Scattered across the world

It was difficult for the government to keep track of Kinder movement during the war. A large number of British children had been evacuated to escape German bombs, and many Kinder had moved with them. Lots of Kinder stayed in the UK after the war was over, and married British citizens. Others decided to make new lives for themselves abroad, in places such as Italy, Jerusalem or Palestine. Wherever they lived, the Kinder became useful members of their adopted countries. They gained important jobs in science, education and the arts. Since World War II, four Kinder have become Nobel Prize winners.

Walter Kohn came to England on the Kindertransport. He was awarded the Nobel Prize for Chemistry in 1998.

Few happy endings

Very few Kinder were lucky enough to be reunited with their parents, who might have run from the Nazis, been killed in war, or sent to concentration camps. The Red Cross sent letters to all Kinder whose parents were known to be dead. Many Jews were still missing and their children had to accept the fact that they would never see them again, or get a chance to say goodbye. Those whose parents were still alive often had to wait years to hear any news, or travel to far-off countries to meet them.

Records such as this one detailed the last known whereabouts of the Kinder's families.

The Kindertransport Association

London hosted the first Kindertransport reunion in 1989. A thousand Kinder took part and introduced each other to their families. Two years later the Kindertransport Association was formed. This non-profit organisation unites Kinder with their living relatives.

Glossary

Anti-Semitism The discrimination against and hatred of Jews.

Bunks A type of bed where one bed is stacked on top of another.

Concentration camps Camps built to hold Germany's prisoners, usually in terrible conditions. They later became death camps and their prisoners were executed.

Deported To be forcibly removed or expelled from a country.

House of Commons One of two houses of Parliament where elected Members of Parliament meet and debate new laws. The other house is the House of Lords.

Internment camp A camp where 'enemy aliens' and prisoners of war are kept.

Kosher Food that can be eaten under Jewish law. Pork, for example, is not allowed.

The Military Cross An award granted to British soldiers for great bravery.

Propaganda Information and rumours spread on a large scale to harm a person or group.

Rabbi A Jewish teacher and religious leader.

The Red Cross An international organisation that aims to prevent human suffering.

Refugees People forced to leave their own country because of war or persecution.

Star of David A common Jewish symbol. It is made of two overlapping triangles.

Synagogue A Jewish house of worship.

U-boat A German submarine. The literal translation is 'undersea boat'.

Further reading

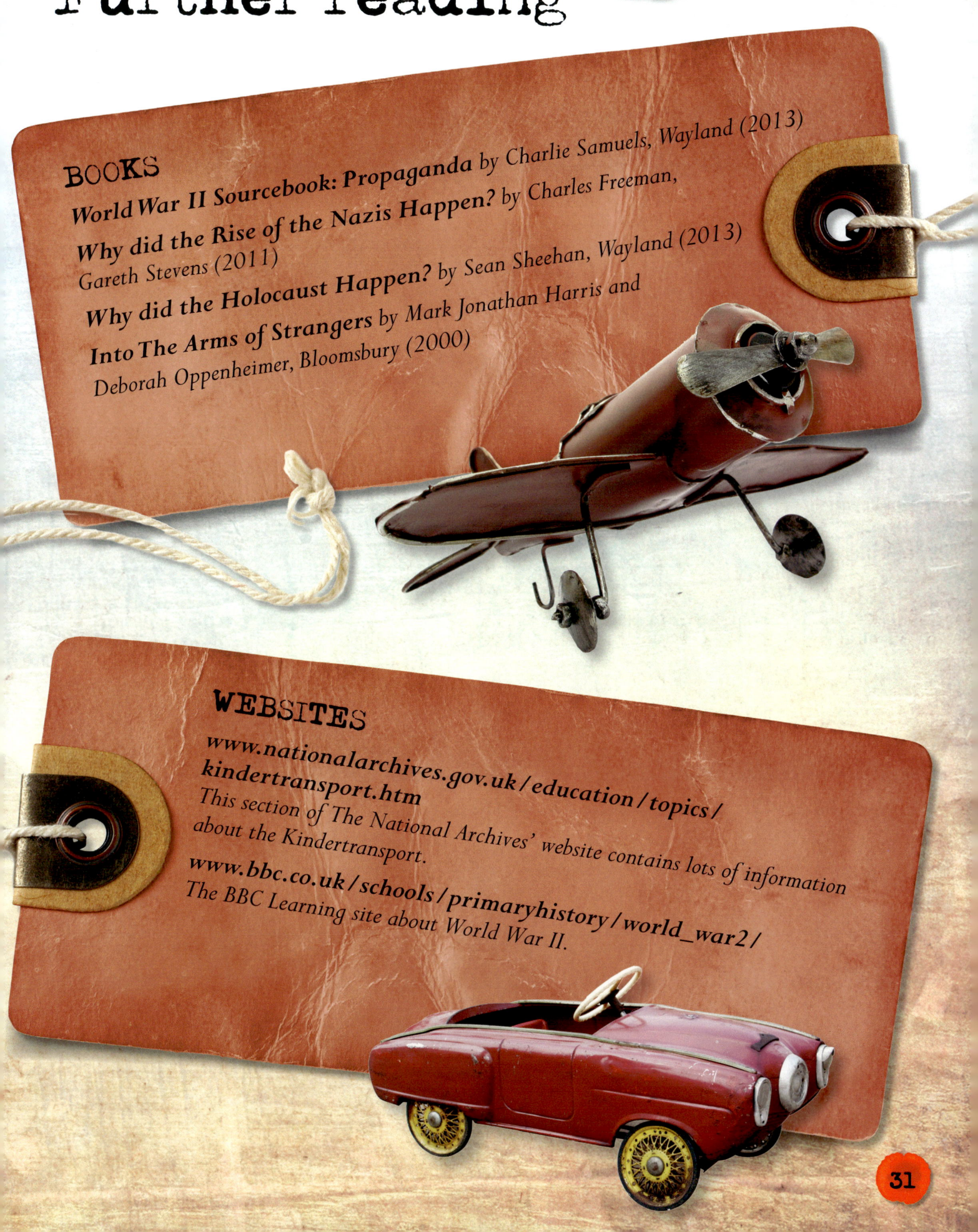

BOOKS

World War II Sourcebook: Propaganda by Charlie Samuels, Wayland (2013)

Why did the Rise of the Nazis Happen? by Charles Freeman, Gareth Stevens (2011)

Why did the Holocaust Happen? by Sean Sheehan, Wayland (2013)

Into The Arms of Strangers by Mark Jonathan Harris and Deborah Oppenheimer, Bloomsbury (2000)

WEBSITES

www.nationalarchives.gov.uk/education/topics/kindertransport.htm
This section of The National Archives' website contains lots of information about the Kindertransport.

www.bbc.co.uk/schools/primaryhistory/world_war2/
The BBC Learning site about World War II.

Index

anti-Semitism 4, 30
Austria 5, 10, 14

Belgium 10, 12, 22
boats & ships (see also ferries) 5, 22, 25
British government 8, 9, 15, 20, 22, 24, 25, 26, 29

camps 12, 13, 16-17, 18, 20
  Dovercourt 12, 13, 14-15
  Engeham 19
  Lowestoft 12, 15
Christians 5, 11
clothes 11, 15, 19, 20
concentration camps 7, 10, 28, 29, 30
Czechoslovakia 5, 12, 13

England 11, 12, 13, 18, 22, 24
entertainment 16, 17
evacuation 5, 29

farms and farming 13, 19, 21
ferries 10, 12
food 15, 16, 17, 18, 20, 25
foster care 9, 13, 18
France 24

Germany 4, 5, 8, 10, 12, 22, 24
Gorell, Lord 26
Great Britain 4, 5, 8, 12, 18, 20, 22, 24, 25, 27, 29
Guardianship Act 26, 28

Hitler, Adolf 4, 5, 6, 24
Holocaust 23
houses 17, 18

identity cards 9, 11
internment camps 24, 25, 30

Jews 4, 5, 6, 7, 8, 9, 18, 20
  bullying 6, 20

deaths 5, 7, 23
deportation 7
religion 20, 21
segregation 6-7
jobs 6, 8, 18, 19, 21, 27, 29

Kindertransport Association 29
Kristallnacht 4, 5, 7, 9

language 16, 21, 27
laws 4, 6, 7, 26, 28
London 10, 18, 20
Luftwaffe 22, 30
luggage 11

marriage 7, 29
medicine 6, 14

Nazi Party 4, 5, 6, 7, 8, 10, 11, 13, 22, 23, 24, 27, 29
Netherlands, the 10, 12, 22
newspapers 6, 9, 19, 26
Nuremberg Law 7

orphans 10, 12

parents 5, 10, 11, 26, 28, 29
planes 12
Poland 5, 7
propaganda 6, 30

Quakers 5, 10, 11

radio 6, 9
Refugee Children's Movement (RCM) 5, 9, 10, 11, 16, 21, 22, 26

Schonfeld, Solomon 20
schools 6, 7, 9, 13, 15, 20, 21
sponsors 9, 13, 16, 18
spying 24
Star of David 6, 30
synagogues 4, 7, 21, 30

trains 5, 6, 10, 11, 12, 18, 22

USA, the 12, 13

Victory in Europe (VE) Day 28

Winton, Nicholas 13
World War I 5, 8, 26
World War II 4, 5, 14, 20, 22, 27, 28, 29

32